D1068427

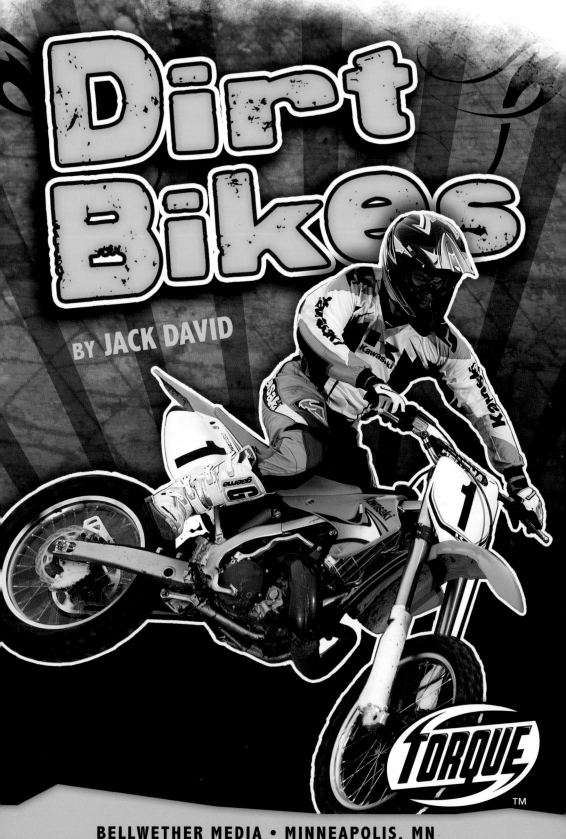

Dirt Bikes

BY JACK DAVID

BELLWETHER MEDIA • MINNEAPOLIS, MN

TORQUE™

Are you ready to take it to the extreme? Torque books thrust you into the action-packed world of sports, vehicles, and adventure. These books may include dirt, smoke, fire, and dangerous stunts.

WARNING: READ AT YOUR OWN RISK.

This edition first published in 2008 by Bellwether Media.

No part of this publication may be reproduced in whole or in part without written permission of the publisher. For information regarding permission, write to Bellwether Media Inc., Attention: Permissions Department, Post Office Box 19349, Minneapolis, MN 55419.

Library of Congress Cataloging-in-Publication Data

David, Jack, 1968–
  Dirt bikes / by Jack David.
     p. cm. — (Torque—cool rides)
  Summary: "Amazing photography accompanies engaging information about dirt bikes. The combination of high-interest subject matter and light text is intended for students in grades 3 through 7"—Provided by publisher.
  Includes bibliographical references and index.
  ISBN-13: 978-1-60014-147-8 (hardcover : alk. paper)
  ISBN-10: 1-60014-147-1 (hardcover : alk. paper)
  1. Trail bikes--Juvenile literature. I. Title.
  TL441.D369 2008
  629.227′5—dc22   2007040561

Contents

What Is a Dirt Bike?

Most motorcycles are built for the road. Dirt bikes are built to go everywhere but the road. Dirt bikes are light, tough, and fast. They can handle dirt, mud, sand, and almost any type of **terrain**.

Dirt bikes can climb mountains and cruise through deserts. Some people race them and do tricks on them. Many people also like to ride them just for fun.

Fast Fact

Trigger Gumm set the world record for the longest jump on a dirt bike when he jumped 277.5 feet (84.5 meters) in Australia on May 17, 2005.

Dirt Bike History

The first motorcycles were built in the late 1800s. One early model was the cross-country motorcycle. This was the earliest dirt bike. People loved to race cross-country motorcycles in dirt races called scrambles.

9

Dirt bikes kept growing in popularity. Soldiers rode them on missions during World War II. The sport of **motocross** racing became popular in the 1960s. **Enduro** racing, **supercross**, and other dirt bike events soon followed. It soon seemed as if dirt bikes were everywhere.

Fast FaCt

A German man named Gottlieb Daimler built one of the first motorcycles. It was called the "boneshaker" because it gave such a rough ride.

11

Parts Of a Dirt Bike

All dirt bikes share some common features. Every bike has a strong metal frame called a **chassis**. Body panels and **fenders** connect to the chassis.

The **suspension system** connects the chassis to the wheels. It is made up of springs and shock absorbers. The suspension system absorbs the rough ride that comes from riding over uneven ground.

Fast FaCt

Dirt bikes sit high off the ground. This is so the bottom of the chassis doesn't hit the ground as the bike bounces over rough trails.

Fast Fact

The Dakar Rally covers thousands of miles through northwest Africa. The race is more than 7,000 miles (11,270 kilometers) long!

Dirt bike tires have deep tread. The bumps and grooves of tread give dirt bikes a good grip on rough surfaces. Dirt bike tires are tough. They have to handle a lot of rough ground without going flat.

Dirt bikes can have either two-**stroke** or four-stroke engines. Two-stroke engines give more raw power. Four-stroke engines create less air pollution and get better **fuel mileage** than two-stroke engines.

Four-Stroke Engine

Two-Stroke Engine

Dirt Bikes in ACtiOn

There are many different kinds of dirt bike races. Enduro races are long, off-road events. Supercross and motocross races take place on dirt courses with lots of jumps and turns. Thousands of fans turn out for the biggest races.

19

Motocross freestyle is also a growing sport.
Riders in this sport do daring stunts such as
backflips on their dirt bikes.

Dirt bikes also have many uses beyond racing and riding for fun. Some cowboys use them to herd animals. Park rangers may use them to get to hard-to-reach places in mountains or forests. A dirt bike can go almost anywhere.

Glossary

chassis–the metal frame of a dirt bike

enduro–an event in which riders navigate long endurance courses; an enduro race often lasts several hours.

fender–a body panel that covers part of a wheel

fuel mileage–the average number of miles a vehicle can travel on a gallon of fuel

motocross–a sport in which riders race dirt bikes on outdoor dirt courses

stroke–the movement of a piston in a cylinder; pistons in two-stroke engines move up and down twice each time a spark plug fires while pistons in four-stroke engines move up and down four times.

supercross–a sport in which riders race dirt bikes on indoor dirt courses

suspension system–the springs and shock absorbers that connect the body of a dirt bike to its wheels

terrain–the natural surface features of the land

To Learn More

AT THE LIBRARY

David, Jack. *Motocross Cycles*. Minneapolis, Minn.: Bellwether, 2008.

Dayton, Connor. *Dirt Bikes*. New York: PowerKids Press, 2007.

Doeden, Matt. *Dirt Bikes*. Mankato, Minn.: Capstone, 2005.

ON THE WEB

Learning more about dirt bikes is as easy as 1, 2, 3.

1. Go to www.factsurfer.com

2. Enter "dirt bikes" into search box.

3. Click the "Surf" button and you will see a list of related web sites.

With factsurfer.com, finding more information is just a click away.

Index

The images in this book are reproduced through the courtesy of: Kawasaki Motors Corporation, front cover, p. 10; American Honda Motor Co., Inc., pp. 5, 6; R. Archer/KTM Sportmotorcycle AG, pp. 7, 18; Sherman/Stringer/Getty Images, p. 9; Horace Abrahams/Stringer/Getty Images, p. 11; Yamaha Motor Corporation, pp. 13, 17; American Suzuki Motor Corporation, pp. 14-15; KTM Sportmotorcycle AG, p. 16; Bakke/Shazamm/ESPN Images, p. 20; Richard Olsenlus/Contributor/National Geographic/Getty Images, p. 21.